Event Boundaries

Also by April Ossmann

Anxious Music

Event Boundaries

April Ossmann

Four Way Books
Tribeca

For my family, present, and past,
in memory of Michael.

Please direct all inquiries to:
Editorial Office
Four Way Books
POB 535, Village Station
New York, NY 10014
www.fourwaybooks.com

811.6
OSSMANN

Library of Congress Cataloging-in-Publication Data

Names: Ossmann, April, author.
Title: Event boundaries / April Ossmann.
Description: New York, NY : Four Way Books, [2017]
Identifiers: LCCN 2016034897 | ISBN 9781935536857 (pbk. : alk. paper)
Classification: LCC PS3615.S634 A6 2017 | DDC 811/.6--dc23
LC record available at https://lccn.loc.gov/2016034897
This book is manufactured in the United States of America and printed on acid-free paper.

Four Way Books is a not-for-profit literary press. We are grateful for the assistance
we receive from individual donors, public arts agencies, and private foundations.

This publication is made possible with public funds from the New York State Council on the Arts,
a state agency.

We are a proud member of the Community of Literary Magazines and Presses.

Distributed by University Press of New England
One Court Street, Lebanon, NH 03766

Contents

I.

II.

III.

I.

One night,

it may be otherwise,
　　but tonight, I see the fawn
in time to slow,

I don't kill
　　or maim it visibly, though
my light terrifies, the fawn

loping awkwardly along
　　the yellow line, fast
as its thin new legs

can wobble it,
　　and I, witness
to suffering

too brightly lit, no sign
　　of its mother, just me,
godlike in deadly metal—

rending silence
　　with my awful horn,
my relentless pursuit—

just me and the fawn, alone
　　on the merciless road
in the immense darkness

we humans reduce
　　to a syllable, as if we could,
or should.

Guaranteed Ten-Minute Oil Change

Give us oil-dark hands flashing
   in dim light, stained waiting chairs,

smoky air and incessant traffic—
   even that all-day whine's

phantom echo in our ears all night—
   but not Larry's tears or fainting,

misfiring language and motor skills.
   Yes, to a successful change

of oil, to the capable
   chain-smoking manager

of our performance-awarded
   regional team,

but not his bending knees
   and un-drunk stumbling—

wavery mirror we wish to see
   no selves in, least of all our own.

Scrim

All I ask of wit
   is that it stand
between me and mystery,
   not like a guard or armor,
more like a screen
   against bites and stings,
a curtain, opaque at night,
   sheer in daylight, swaying
in wind, offering glimpses
   of destiny, a jester singing
into the abyss as my ship
   sinks into the Arctic,
strumming a lute
   as a lightning strike
burns the only home
   I've ever known, punning
and humming in darkness,

as I heat my hands

over the embers, as if

that last warmth matters.

Venture

Early spring, earth
a brown wound

too little green hopes
to heal, we venture

drinking sloppy coffee
from a single cup,

stopping on the interstate
to watch migrating hawks.

You swear you can't
share a bed with anyone,

your sense of freedom
to sleep, wake, curl up

or sprawl, disturbed
by that other rhythm—

but I wake each night
while you sleep,

to find us aligned:
traveling together

in the dark flight
toward morning.

Stubborn

I know it'll be hard after the blizzard,
but don't ponder it. You can't,
if you plan to act. Where would
Hercules, Ulysses, or any heroes be

if they'd thought? Take Superman.
Could he have flown? So I'm stuck,
hip-deep and rabid, talking
myself out from where the plow

left gray-flecked snow banked
too deep for me: calm down—
lift one ski, then the other...
soon, I'm in a rhythm—

not easy, but any rhythm's
easier than breaking stride.
I've had relationships like that,
tight as outgrown shoes—

so it's not fun, but a challenge
I can't resist. White pines loaded
with snow threaten, creaking in wind,
but I pretend not to hear.

Only half my usual distance,
but I turn homeward,
sweat-soaked, creeped-out
by the doomsday yellow overcast.

It occurs to me I could die lying
under a blank birch,
gone blanker with snow, though
I can't picture it. Like most, I'd *like*

to go sleeping, but forecast drama:
plane crash, earthquake, something
with explosions and companions
or an audience, something unlike

these deserted woods drifted white,
June-deep already at mid-winter—
will I finally get my fill of snow?
I moved here for it,

and every winter, I'm disappointed.
It's never like novels, where flakes
keep falling till people are bored,
scared, or homicidal.

It seems I like my thrills at home—
alcoholic, depressed, bipolar?
Send 'em over. No job too tough
for this little prairie dog. Like Laura,

in *The Long Winter*, I'm the latest
in a long line of headstrong women—
square-jawed and stubborn, convinced
we'll win through to spring.

The Doubt House

The hill our house is on
　　seems steeper each day,
and the house shifts uneasily
　　on its foundation. Trees
lean as I walk, and I hear
　　strange new animals
in the woods. Something
　　is splitting mountain into rock
with great haste—
　　strewing angular fragments
on the ground,
　　filling the brook
with sharp teeth
　　as it widens, creeping
toward the house—
　　yesterday, one face,
today another.
　　Tomorrow, I may wake
to a stranger.

Infidelity

I never stopped to consider
its less illicit pleasures:

its syllables tumbling so readily
off the tongue, the tongue

slapping lightly, repeatedly,
the roof of the mouth, the mouth

left open, as if with expectation,
or in surprise, or song—this solo

which leaves you alone,
holding the final note.

The Terror of Doors

No one considers the door's terror,
    held so tenuously
by such flimsy hinges, longing

    for an axis so awe-inspiring
only its god could open it,
    avoiding endless submission

to the careful and careless alike—
    the sideways swinging fall
as the universe shoulders in,

    slamming the door
against the wall.
    Doors want to stay

in a frame's familiar embrace—
    though one rebel
slanted and swelled,

    refusing the fit,
preferring to stay
    where its bottom found a seat

on the equally unruly floor—
    and a querulous door
sometimes bangs so deliberately

    in unperceived breezes,
as to unnerve its owners
    with seeming agency,

an urge to escape its fate
        and go winging off
after something

        unimaginable in space—
the knob turned beak
        or aeronautical control stick

to steer past stars,
        the frame abandoned
to examine its navel;

        and the wall, never elated
by the hole put in it,
        now, a toothless mouth,

a rectangular *O*
        of awe or terror, as the gods
of chance advance.

Loves Me, Loves Me Not

Whoever invented
that particular violence—
stripping one by one,
the original daisy's petals,
and finding an answer
in injury, was right.

Where the Wolves Are

after Jeanann Verlee

I embody no appetite more epic
   than the chickadee's

dipping, diving trajectory:
   the black-capped bird's hungers,

no less urgent than mine—constant,
   propelling flight, drawing him

surely to my feeder, his snacking on seed
   not meant to please me, my eyelashes

are birds, my hands are wolves—
   subsuming the human; avian aerobatics,

bold as lupine howling—
   the wolves' hunger is all our existence:

where the wolves are is where I live,
   their lingering, contralto wails,

my reprise, just as the chickadee's
   homing dives mirror my grasping hands.

How Like a Dog

Because he likes cats,
he doesn't realize how like a dog

he pets her—with the patience
bordering on impatience

one allots a too affectionate dog;
petting and worrying

she might do something distasteful
or inappropriate—lick his legs, drool,

or show an unwelcome interest
in his crotch, when all he wants

is to leave with his conscience clear:
she wants affection; he grants it.

She, like any dog, knows the rules
of *this* game: gratitude

for any stick thrown,
however feebly.

Mars Rising

after Gwendolyn Brooks

An insistent tapping leads us to a window to see an
ardent sight, an agile, determined bird, indignant,
at the unremitting violation of his claim, this fervid robin's
leaping repeatedly from the sill to peck his reflection, resolute
in his intention—on every ledge his dripping white donation.

A City, Like Venice

You love like *The Boy in the Plastic
        Bubble*, the movie about a baby

born with no immune system,
        entirely susceptible to injury.

The rest of us trust existence
        more or less as we proceed—

unlike the infant,
        a flu or infected wound

won't mean the end for us.
        They raised him in the bubble

to save him for more of the same.
        He finally burst those bonds

to spend himself—
        but you're still saving.

Your courtly demeanor
        armors like protective plastic,

in the airport's too-open atrium,
        as you try not to think about

what's irking me, or might be.
        I see the built-in gloves

his bubble came equipped with:
   reaching for his parents,

pathetic expressions flattened
   to grotesque by the plastic wall,

their filtered warmth
   the closest he comes to embrace.

Climbing hand-over-hand, I have done
   what none of those airport strangers

eyeing your grace in that artificial light
   will ever do: I've trespassed finally,

your noisome moats, feet-thick walls,
   and battlements; I have found

what they hid: a city, like Venice,
   just barely kept from drowning.

Celestial Solo, or Divine Funk?

after Gwendolyn Brooks

I think it must be lonely to be God, unmarried for eternity, but I
would much rather imagine her serene and content, than think
she wouldn't enjoy her freedom from the mundane, chuckling, as it
pursues us like a hungry puppy needing constant feeding. She must
be as fully entertained as a snake swallowing a mouse whole can be—
celestial music always at the ready, never angry or surly or lonely,
no toilets to scrub, hair to gray or breasts to sag, no harm or death to
dread, no loss of love to suffer—spiritually evolved as a being can be—
though an eternity without orgasms must make it lonely to be God.

Hearing That Music

The song I think of as my shower song
isn't mine, but his—extolling the wisdom

of living in the present, accompanied
by synthesized orchestral music—

the kind of melody attending
a lyrical foray into the past,

countered by chords charging
the future—a song triangled

by anticipation, fulfillment, regret:
the sweet, elaborate stasis he lives for—

the moment I can't tolerate
before decision, when he feels rich

with choices, so many, only all
or none could be correct.

He's played it so often, he knows
I'll protest if he plays it again,

so he listens while I shower.
Though he's away, I hear it now,

and stop the water, pausing half-rinsed
and shivering, to hear the call more clearly.

All or Nothing

The red dog waits daily for quarry:
any vehicle drawing even with the driveway

draws her lunging, barking chase—
legs blur as if her four-paw power

might best four cylinders,
inhaling dusty wakes as we might lilac

or baking bread or ocean breeze—
her ambition so immense, we can only imagine

what she'll do if she attains it—
adrenalin rush stopped dead

and forward motion foiled—
will she overshoot her target

before skidding to a stop
to inspect her prize?

Will she find it less enticing
at biting distance,

the scratched and faded paint
all too apparent? Will she shrug

her canine shoulders and walk away
to await a bigger, newer car—

a more perfectly realized desire
or a more perfect striving?

Reveille

Awake, passersby!
    Lilies aim flaming bugles—
trumpeting July.

II.

Duet

The wipers move together
only in adversity,
one always leading,
while the other lags.
They travel in concert,
the distance
between them constant.
They lie together only
in sleep,
when they lie as if dead.

His Mother's Hair

The last time he cut his mother's hair,
   the rude morning sun
left no corner of her kitchen private,
   the light surgically clean
where it fell on his scissors.
   Her hair fell in a blonde circle
on the lake blue tile—smell of coffee
   and cinnamon; her laughing
shook her head, *Hold still*, he said,
   his hands surfeit with the curl
and softness of her hair.

   Three weeks after her death,
a stranger entered the salon
   and settled in the chair.
She had the color and shape
   of his mother's hair,
and when he sunk his hands in it,
   the texture, even cowlicks,
individual as freckles—same.
   Twice he had to leave the room,
and twice, he returned—still,
   when he touched her hair, it blurred.
Hold still, he said, *hold still*.

This Blue

Dearest, today the sky is so blue
   it hurts. Blue like the red

of my blood, like the orange
   of oranges. Blue as sleeping

on clean sheets, more Swiss
   chocolate than I can eat—

could anything real
   be so perfectly blue?

It makes me feel too full
   and unbearably empty.

November's thousand browns,
   varied grays and evergreens

seem superreal against it.
   I fear this blue's a debt

I can't repay: a Mercedes, Rolls,
   Cadillac. Take it back. Like you,

it's too wide, too deep, too blue—
   it's too much. It's not enough.

Bounty

The year the perennial beds
  finally filled in:

year of abundance—
  year of yearning,

wishing every flower
  a longer bloom—

longing, perversely,
  to begin again from nothing,

build the garden up
  from soil so barren it isn't—

so merely sand and powder
  even weeds disdain it—

work to make knuckles
  callus-knobby,

to abrade the knees
  and give the body a thirst

no nectar will quench; work
  to earn a lassitude surpassing

the post-coital in pleasure;
   rise eager again to labor—

smash the happy-meter
   to smithereens!

Turning Forty: What I Say, What I Know

I say no sex is worth dying for, no man
worth living *with*—nevermind *for*—
I say *Caution* comma is my new first name,
my old first name, my last—
I say not even Death will know me.

I know the first bite of any apple's best,
the one the mouth's juices leap to meet,
whose sweet sting laves the tongue's ache,
the bite against which hunger breaks—
and the pleasure of being bitten.

Wildlife Central

Nevermind the garden:
chipmunks tunneling
my perennials,
star-nosed moles,
and a well-fed groundhog,
all tunneling my lawn.
What irks me is the robin's
aggressive daily pecking
of my windows,
the woodpecker
hammering my metal roof,
the sparrow nesting
in my dryer vent pipe—
but mostly, the few hundred
mice who've taken up
residence in my walls
and crawl space,
skittering day and night
about their business,
leaving feces enough
to fertilize a garden—
falling down interior walls
and dying, reeking
for weeks as they rot,
breeding blow-fly
infestations...
the exterminator's left
multiple kinds of death traps
and they're dying
by the dozens,
but the supply's

so seemingly endless,
I've begun to wonder
who belongs here:
just this week—
dead, alas,
since they eat mice—
I found an ermine
in my cellar.

Stupid

Injuries are, mostly.
There's a moment, lucid and still
as a Sunday in June, when you know—

but do it anyway, like running
in rain down steep trails
jumbled with roots and rocks—

like grabbing the wire just now
getting caught in the mower's
whirling blade. Later, nursing

your cut, break or sprain,
you'll remember it and curse yourself.
Or consider *lust*: my body's got

no more sense than a bitch in heat.
She'd just as soon roll over for a bookie
as a banker, or a good-sized mutt.

And how about *decisions*?
Based on some imaginary future
which neither you nor I

have the wisdom to imagine
correctly. And then more decisions
based on decisions based

on false imaginary futures.
And *intelligence*? Dimmest bulb
in the building. *It thinks it's smart,*

thinks it can decide who to love
and whether or not to bed the Ex.
The truth is, intelligence

thought lust made the decision
which caused the injuries,
but it was stupid all the time.

Protest

I didn't know goutweed
    existed till I had it,
smothering better perennials.
    Now I see it invading woods,
conquering fields.

All these years here,
    and this is the first
I've noticed spent leaves falling
    in spring.

How can trees already
    be dispersing their dead
like so many ashes—

    or do weak leaves
abandon their branches
    to strengthen the tribe?

Have I missed it
    through inattention
or denial—

    or do these leaves
know something
    others don't? June
is too soon for doom.

Spare me the sight
of green leaves dying,
  the thunder
of each leaf landing,

 their shredding
in the maw
 of the equally
ruthless mower.

Dark Chocolate

She smells like herself again,

all of me washed, I hope reluctantly,

away. We embrace with a hint

of the military, though who's

the soldier, I couldn't say.

Slow missile, I aim my car toward

another state's dark reaches,

and begin to calculate my ETA,

absently lick my too-dry lips—

the last remnant of shared dark chocolate—sweet

and sharp on the tip of my tongue

which, avoiding collision—

I bite hard enough to bleed.

Winter of Descent

Winter of my knee surgery,
    of recovering just in time
to injure my shoulder,
    shoveling all the snow
I ever wished for as a child—
    winter I learned
what that much snow meant
    to a middle-aged body, intent,
on shifting it too swiftly aside;
    winter of my dear, obedient body,
all too willing to ignore injury
    at the mind's persnickety command;
too willing a wife
    to its unsparing husbandry:
it took injury to teach
    this husband patience;
this long, slow, winter of learning
    a new content;
this winter of de-motion.

Pique

The wood pecker isn't pecking wood,
    he's pecking the metal eave
of my standing seam roof,
    making a racket that reverberates
as echo: strutting his stuff
    for a female more piqued
than I—or staking territory
    we disagree is his, an argument
I've had with one or two
    of his human fellows.
But who doesn't want
    to beat on something once
in a while—who doesn't
    miss metal trash can lids,
the opportunity to perfect
    the perfect clamor?
Take a bat, make some noise:
    give some ears what for,
ring them inside out.

Taking the Argument for a Walk

A frigid wind tears our eyes,
    waves rebuke the beach,
        and relent, rebuke and relent,

seeming to hiss *adiós*,
    as they go…each frothing
        second thought subsumed.

Just ocean and more ocean,
    gray as far as we can see—
        and no lightening of sky.

Not a day for wading,
    and it wouldn't aid efforts
        at a closer view, nor would

sailing a boat avail us—
    unattainable destination
        receding as we seek it:

another horizon where earth
    only appears to join heaven,
        one more imaginary division

to argue—or ponder—
    our unhealing wound
        a split only we can suture.

When Your People Call My People to Arrange a Meeting

Know that lately,
  I am giving myself

to sleep as I once
  gave myself in love,

my body flung eagerly
  into bed; limbs limp and heavy

with pleasure; the bedclothes
  on waking arranged exactly

as I entered them.
  I am in love now

with rest, with release
  from the tireless ego—

let us meet while we sleep
  (which seems lately to be less

a rehearsal for death,
  than a preview

of immortality), and see
  what our souls see,

where we are
  our inward selves only,

and all our selves
  are not at war—

when all our loyalty
  belongs to dreaming.

The Mechanical Home Care Bed

An awkward unbeautiful ferry,

too big for the room it sailed in—

whose slanting metal bars

did nothing to keep the rough sea out,

but appeared to keep my father in,

clinging as he did to one

with his too-thin arm,

and tilting his gaze

to see around them: such

a transforming, grateful smile

for an offering so small: such

mundane conversation. The bed

with its hanging trapeze—

a sailing circus none of us wanted

to witness—intended they said,

to assist in raising himself

from the bed, though we knew

the truth: a hangman's triangular

noose dangling all those weeks

over his weary head.

Table for One

He imagines she's boiling water for tea—
he, just sitting to beer and ribs.

He recalls her kettle doesn't whistle or sing
as she does, just risks boiling over—

it's like her, he muses, to have a kettle like that,
to think her singing strength enough.

The beer obligingly beads the frost off the glass,
and his ribs have cooled just enough for handling...

they lie so willingly on the plate, he can't
bring himself to address them till he's tried

to bend one, just to feel some resistance, as God did,
with Eve—now *those* were ribs with a spine!

She's boiling water, he, just sitting—each
lonely as an apple left to winter on the branch.

III.

Training for the Apocalypse

Thirty million people in the path
of a snowstorm little more
than nothing, that might
have been something
beyond endless parsing
of each possible apocalypse
imagined and averted—
just this once, by the grace
of whatever god
you're praying to
(ours, we devotedly hope),
have we avoided the tragedy
of three feet of unwelcome snow
slowing our coming and going.

Losing Reason

Intuition says it would be
    like entering a parking garage—
that moment of blindness
    when sun and shadow meet;

the millisecond
    we never remember
between conscious thought
    and sleep;

the last instant before
    orgasm when the conscious
stops watching;

    the arc of that final
missed step before falling before
    you know you're falling, except
the falling wouldn't end.

Mayhem Meditation

No one will protect you from mayhem.
Not your nuclear power company,
promising safe, clean, efficient power;
nor your power-hungry government;
and most assuredly, not *unsurence*.
Whatever brand insurance you have
will likely cover a smidgeon
of the replacement,
and none of the clean-up costs,
once you've won your war
with the company determining
whether they're obligated
to pay you even a fraction
of what you've paid them,
but as far as the mayhem itself goes,
you're alone with whatever your god
or upbringing or DNA gave you:
fortitude, equanimity or ungainly,
video-enhanced floundering.
So, tell us: how do you feel,
watching your home go six feet under?
Could you cry a little, for the camera?

Event Boundaries

Such a comfort to know
       it's temporary dementia,

when I enter a room
       and forget why I came—

to fetch a pen to write a note
       to remember the task

my brain's just mislaid—
       I've only to pass back

through the fogging doorway
       to reclaim a resolution or name—

and conversely, a relief to think
       I won't have to live

every future tick and tock
       of my anxious watch

recalling how distraught
       I was over anyone's death:

I've only to stroll
       a doorframe's border

to forget a particular grief,
       misbegotten love

or moral lapse, to escape
        the rasp of conscience

or self-flagellation,
        to visit the nations

of remembrance
        or amnesia as I please.

A Good Day in Middle Age

For my beloved
   ones, a temporary stay
of execution.

What Nature Did

She stands perfectly still,
　looking in at me—

or so it seems,
　fifty feet into the woods;

staring and bleeding
　from a wound south

and west of her neck.
　So intent, I think

she must have a message
　or question—

my human side says,
　whether I'll save her

from what error, animal,
　　or human nature did.

I want to carry her to medicine,
　though I know she outweighs me

and would flee, however slowly,
　at my approach. Animal rescue

says they don't do deer,
　but they'll shoot her if I ask—

as will animal control—no one
　agrees with what my conscience

dictates, and I lack
   all relevant medical skills.

She hasn't moved
   her gaze or stance in the hour

given uselessly to pity
   by one of us,

and to who knows what
   by the other,

besides mute bleeding.
   I've failed her, or failed

to get the message,
   but failed either way,

conscience or ego insists.
   I spend the next hour ignoring,

but she doesn't leave
   until I watch her painful progress:

downslope, across the road,
   and finally, out of sight—

except for the haunting one of us
   is foolish enough to host.

3D Feeling

Not just any man,
  a particular love—

was it the man
  or the moment,

each skin cell,
  each neuron,

awake to sensation—
  unmitigated presence,

absence of cognitive
  interference

between desire and divine,
  bed become temple,

and motion, prayer,
  in union too briefly

known as holy—
  science, art and divine

on one side,
  herstory in the making,

the goddess returned—
  for once not parsing

desire's quantum theory,
   channeling abundance

just this once from its god,
   from her heaven

in tousled sheets
   at the base

of the multi-tasking,
   overly intellectual

and bossy brain—
   a holo-moment to frame.

Regarding Hurry

—Craftsbury, Vermont

Folk here move so slowly,

      I felt stymied

at first, as if I'd fallen into

      a new dimension or gravity

preventing speed,

      peopled by alien tribes.

It seemed not so much

      a mindful relaxation,

as a species of resistance

      I couldn't identify

till I'd walked my fill

      of landscape writ large—

dotted, yes, with villages—

      that could only seem ephemeral

in the landscape's vastness

      and eerie ongoingness,

its seeming unconcern.

      Does the landscape care

that I'm in it—or whether

I love or loathe it?

I think I know its answer.

Farmers have been taming it

several hundred years

to little effect: some views

that wouldn't otherwise exist,

but woods encroach

from every side of these doomed

agricultural frontiers.

Woods ruled here

before humans grew crops,

and will again too soon

to make corn a comfort.

Does the earth, saturated

from a week's rain,

welcome my walk?

It seems to, cupping each footstep

with its greedy, slurping suck,

    letting each foot reluctantly loose

before grabbing the other.

    And rain? Just as glad to fall on me

as any man or beast or dwelling—

    though it seems gladdest joining

these brief, noisy streams I imagine

    only exist in spring—

but *do* exist every spring—

    water in such a hurry,

I'd like to know just what the hurry is—

    and don't say *sea* to me,

we're far enough from there,

    with mountains enough between,

I don't see it going anywhere,

    but down or in,

growing a plant or two en route—

    exactly what I'll do one day too soon—

with or without this earthen sponge

     so eager for more feeding—

reason enough, I'll grant,

     for resisting any hurry.

Sigh

April snow bends
    each lilac branch,

heavy and wet
    as your body on mine

after love-making,
    but less warm—

in truth, a better simile
    for loss than love,

though love appears
    predicated on loss—

or the fear of it—
    surely, every new love

predicts new loss—
    branch, you bend

more easily than we,
    but sooner break.

This snow's weeping
    is its vanishing,

but the lilac's sigh of relief
  is not its life—

no breath is ours to keep,
  just as no body is.

After

oxygen failed
to reach his brain, maybe
strains of the Lynyrd Skynyrd
he loved lofted over the street,
Free Bird with no one there
to tame or change it—maybe
it annoyed a neighbor weary
of hearing its repetition—
a finite irritation, last song
on the album, and no one
left to replay it—maybe
he died in silence he craved
more than sound, soul free
of the interfering ego's
constant harping—free
of what he could not change,
none of us could help him,
he wouldn't change—no one

helped him tie the knots

to make the noose, alcohol

changed him in ways

not even he could know—

of the last of this man's life,

who so loved company—

all we know is he died alone—

his mind a bird he couldn't change—

can a mind exist without a brain—

no dictionary locates it—

a bird always free to fly—*yes,*

we still remember you—

the coroner said

the noose stopped oxygen—

my brother died alone

at the end of his rope.

Black Comedy for My Brother

In tune with a cell phone's staticky rendering
   of Lynyrd Skynyrd's *Free Bird*,
we cast his ashes in the river, lodged
   in the funeral home's best custom
cardboard bowl, but they don't float
   as they're supposed to—the painted disc plops—
and sinks like every stone I've ever thrown
   in anger or boredom or striving to skip—
in short, like every swan dive
   turned belly flop, every stillborn hope.

Suicide Lament

Adrift on indifferent waves,
    blinded by fog so saturated

it beads and drips
    from every face,

afraid we'll hear
    behind the veil

a chorus of regret
    for the misspent,

a lament-heaven
    of angels wailing

for all they failed to save,
    an eternity

of weeping interspersed
    by celestial music sung

sotto voce, to remind us
    of all we miss—

grief like an ocean
        we're afraid

we'll never reach
        the shore of—

and no lifeboat sailing
        toward our vale.

Reach

The cut tulips bloom

too soon to last

as long as I will them to—

if another's will

could keep one tulip,

brother or parent alive—

what altered world

would we inhabit?

The tulips' mortal wounds

don't prevent their curving—

and re-curving, each time

I shift them in their vase,

seeking, for reasons

I don't understand,

a more perfect symmetry.

The sun rises before I do,

and the tulips—

as if light could save them—

have with their dying reach

arced again beyond

        my will for them, sideways, as far

as their dismembered stems allow,

        into its animating grace

by the time I wake.

Dust to Dust

Nevermind that keeping ashes
   on the mantel feels ghoulish,
and comically impractical:

not just another thing,
   a miniature memento urn, to dust,
but dust to dust—

I dread the conversational
   Hara-kiri, not, *that's what's left
of my brother*, but, *he died of suicide*:

the chasm of silence following the leap—
   so the cremains stay
in the office closet till they migrate

through no will of their own
   to a moving box
I haven't unpacked and likely won't.

Sieve

Young men seem all edges
   and hard angles, shoulders
      like shelves, bellies like slides

to the most obvious
   of pleasures, young women
      all crisp curves, so round

and firm, their union seems
   geometrically insoluble.
      We soften as we age,

our geometries slipping
   and sliding, in small
      or quantum leaps,

bodies and definitions blurring
   as we morph, like mercury,
      into each new self we shape.

Living softens us
   to fill death's vessel,
      not like the solid we seem,

but the liquid we are—
   so we may slip the cup
      like the sieve it is.

O, *Chicago*, O'Hare

One among the shifting mass
  of humanity intent
on countless destinations,
  one hungry stomach

and dry mouth among many,
  one brain dazed
by the speed and altitude
  of flights unnatural

to any animal, by herding,
  followed by waiting,
succeeded by rushing,
  waiting, herding—

and more flight
  incomprehensible
to any body contained
  in this seemingly unwieldy

mass of metal lifting
  improbably over Chicago,
where a misty orange aura
  hovers over the city's

brighter lights, as if
  its soul sought ascension
it could only attempt,
  as if the aura

might break free
  and follow us,
wherever we might fly,
  wheresoever we may rest—

one with the multitude
  of humans en route
through mystery,
  to mystery.

Acknowledgments

Grateful acknowledgment is made to the editors of the journals and anthologies who first published poems in this collection, sometimes in earlier versions.

Berkeley Poetry Review, Connotation Press, Cumberland River Review, From the Fishouse, Folio: A Literary Journal, Georgetown Review, Inertia Magazine, Interim, The Laurel Review, New England Review, MiPO Magazine, Pamp~le~Mousse, Prairie Schooner, Santa Clara Review, The Spoon River Poetry Review, Talking River, and *Valparaiso Poetry Review.*

"Infidelity" also appeared in *From the Fishouse: An Anthology of Poems that Sing, Rhyme, Resound, Syncopate, Alliterate, and Just Plain Sound Great,* edited by Matt O'Donnell, Camille Dungy, Jeff Thomson (Persea Books).

Heartfelt thanks to the Vermont Arts Council and the National Endowment for the Arts, and to The Writers Center in Craftsbury, Vermont, directed by Julia Shipley, for the funds, time and space essential to my writing of this work, and to Kevin Goodan for editorial assistance. "Regarding Hurry" is dedicated to Julia, and "His Mother's Hair," to Joseph. "One night" owes a tip of the hat to Jane Kenyon and Chase Twichell; "Where the Wolves Are," to Jeanann Verlee; and "The Doubt House," to Alice B. Fogel. "Mayhem Meditation" is in conversation with Allstate's mayhem commercials featuring Dean Winters, and "After" is in conversation with the lyrics to Lynyrd Skynyrd's "Free Bird." "Mars Rising" and "Celestial Solo, or Divine Funk?" are Golden Shovel tributes to Gwendolyn Brooks.

April Ossmann is the author of *Anxious Music* (Four Way Books) and has published her poetry widely in journals and anthologies, including *Colorado Review, New England Review,* and *From the Fishouse* (Persea Books). Her poetry awards include a Vermont Arts Council Creation Grant, and a *Prairie Schooner* Readers' Choice Award. She has published essays including *Thinking Like an Editor: How to Order Your Poetry Manuscript* (*Poets & Writers*, March/April 2011), and a biography/critical study of poet Lynda Hull in *American Writers Supplement XXI* (Charles Scribner's Sons, 2011). Former Executive director of Alice James Books (2000 – 2008), she owns a consulting business (www.aprilossmann.com) offering manuscript editing and publishing advice. She is an Editor-in-Residence for the low-residency MFA in Creative Writing Program at Sierra Nevada College, and teaches private tutorials and poetry workshops using a method she developed to teach poets to revise their work objectively. She lives in West Windsor, Vermont.

Publication of this book was made possible by grants and donations. We are also grateful to those individuals who participated in our 2016 Build a Book Program. They are:

Anonymous (8), Evan Archer, Sally Ball, Jan Bender-Zanoni, Zeke Berman, Kristina Bicher, Carol Blum, Lee Briccetti, Deirdre Brill, Anthony Cappo, Carla & Steven Carlson, Maxwell Dana, Machi Davis, Monica Ferrell, Martha Webster & Robert Fuentes, Dorothy Goldman, Lauri Grossman, Steven Haas, Mary Heilner, Henry Israeli, Christopher Kempf, David Lee, Jen Levitt, Howard Levy, Owen Lewis, Paul Lisicky, Katie Longofono, Cynthia Lowen, Louise Mathias, Nathan McClain, Gregory McDonald, Britt Melewski, Kamilah Moon, Carolyn Murdoch, Tracey Orick, Zachary Pace, Gregory Pardlo, Allyson Paty, Marcia & Chris Pelletiere, Eileen Pollack, Barbara Preminger, Kevin Prufer, Peter & Jill Schireson, Roni & Richard Schotter, Soraya Shalforoosh, Peggy Shinner, James Snyder & Krista Fragos, Megan Staffel, Marjorie & Lew Tesser, Susan Walton, Calvin Wei, Abigail Wender, Allison Benis White, and Monica Youn.